PULLING
DOWN
STRONGHOLDS

DEREK PRINCE

PULLING DOWN STRONGHOLDS

WHITAKER
HOUSE

Publisher's Note: This book was compiled from the extensive archive of Derek Prince's unpublished materials and approved by the Derek Prince Ministries editorial team.

PULLING DOWN STRONGHOLDS

Derek Prince Ministries
P.O. Box 19501
Charlotte, North Carolina 28219-9501
www.derekprince.org

ISBN: 978-1-60374-854-4
eBook ISBN: 978-1-60374-853-7
Printed in the United States of America
© 2013 by Derek Prince Ministries–International

Whitaker House
1030 Hunt Valley Circle
New Kensington, PA 15068
www.whitakerhouse.com

Library of Congress Cataloging-in-Publication Data is available from the publisher.

13 14 **UJ** 24 23 22

CONTENTS

INTRODUCTION

Are you aware that there is an invisible war going on all around you? And are you aware that you are destined to fight in this war?

Two Spiritual Kingdoms in Conflict

The ministry of Jesus Christ on earth demonstrated the basic fact that there are two invisible spiritual kingdoms that are at war with one another: one is the kingdom of God, and the other is the kingdom of Satan.

Even a casual reading of the New Testament reveals, undeniably, that Jesus regularly and effectively engaged in what could be termed "spiritual warfare." It is the purpose of this book to examine the concept of spiritual warfare as a definite, clearly identifiable aspect of Christian living. In the process, we will establish some guidelines to help us wage spiritual war effectively as followers of Jesus Christ.

As a Christian, you would most likely not hesitate to affirm the concept that God has a kingdom. What may be more problematic for you (and what you may not even have been aware of) is the reality that Satan also has a kingdom. Indeed, he does, and it is crucial for you, as a believing Christian, to understand the nature of his kingdom and how it operates.

Drafted into Warfare

If you are a citizen of the kingdom of God through faith in Christ, you are automatically at war with the kingdom of Satan. Many people don't recognize this fact, so let me illustrate the point. Suppose I were a citizen of Australia, and my country went to war, God forbid, with New Zealand. (We trust this sort of conflict would never actually happen!) But if it were so, then as a citizen of Australia, I would automatically be at war with New Zealand, because I would belong to a nation that was at war with another nation.

And so it is for us as citizens of God's kingdom. Since the kingdom of God is at war with the kingdom of Satan, and we are citizens of God's kingdom, then we have no other option—we are inevitably involved in the war with the kingdom of Satan.

Since we are already in this war, let us discover the answer to these basic questions and more: (1) Why is there spiritual warfare? (2) Who is fighting whom? (3) With which side are we aligned? (4) How can we wage spiritual warfare with discernment and effectiveness?

PART I

AN INVISIBLE SPIRITUAL WAR

CHAPTER ONE

OPEN WARFARE

To begin our study on the nature of spiritual warfare, we will examine a passage from Matthew 12. The background to this account is that Jesus had just healed a man by casting out the evil spirit that had caused him to be blind and mute.

The Reality of Evil Spirits

Before we go further, let me point out that even in today's modern world, evil spirits cause people to be blind, deaf, and mute. My wife Ruth and I discovered this reality when we were in Pakistan a number of years ago. Although Pakistan is 98 percent Muslim, God opened a wonderful door of ministry to us and gave us the freedom to hold public meetings. Up to 16,000 people gathered at our meetings. That huge attendance was for one reason alone: they had heard that we would be praying for the sick. That was the sole reason that most of the people came.

In the course of ministering to people at one meeting, Ruth and I plunged into a crowd of men who were standing before us, waiting to receive prayer. One man touched his ears and then touched his tongue. We could not speak his language, but I understood what he was doing: he was showing us that he was deaf and mute. I knew, theoretically, the scriptural thing to do, and so I thought, *I'll do it and see what happens.* I said, "You deaf and dumb spirit that is in this man, I am speaking to you and not to this man. In the name of the Lord Jesus, I command you to come out of him!" Then, I instructed the man, "Now, say something." And immediately, he heard. He didn't understand English, but he could hear my voice, and he began to make sounds. They marched him up to the platform and told the people that he had been delivered from the deaf and mute spirit. And I said to myself, *This approach works!*

For the next ten minutes, Ruth and I went around looking for deaf and mute people—in Pakistan, they are not hard to find. That day, we saw at least ten people delivered from the condition of being deaf and mute when that particular evil spirit was driven out of them. I share this story because deliverance from demon possession is not a theory, nor is it some old-fashioned tradition. It is a living, present reality.

The Kingdom of God Versus the Kingdom of Satan

Returning now to Matthew 12, let us read what happened when Jesus set the pattern for the activity of deliverance, such as Ruth and I ministered in Pakistan:

> *Now when the Pharisees heard it* [that Jesus had delivered a man possessed by a blind and mute spirit] *they said, "This fellow does not cast out demons except by Beelzebub, the ruler of the demons."*   (Matthew 12:24)

The Pharisees made a terrible accusation! They said, in effect, "He can cast out demons because He is in league with the ruler of the demons." Jesus answered them,

> *Every kingdom divided against itself is brought to desolation, and every city or house divided against itself will not stand. If Satan casts out Satan, he is divided against himself. How then will his kingdom stand?*   (Matthew 12:25–26)

In this passage, Jesus stated very clearly that Satan has a kingdom, and that it is not divided. Then He went on to speak about the kingdom of God:

*And if I cast out demons by Beelzebub, by whom
do your sons cast them out? Therefore they shall be
your judges. But if I cast out demons by the Spirit
of God, surely the kingdom of God has come upon
you.* (Matthew 12:27–28)

Through the ministry of delivering people from evil
spirits, the clash between the two kingdoms is brought
right out into the open. In the above passage, the invisible kingdom of Satan is represented by the demons; the
invisible kingdom of God is represented by Jesus—and
we are called to continue His ministry in His name.
(See, for example, John 14:12.)

I believe that Satan particularly fears the ministry
of deliverance for two reasons: First, because, again, it
brings his invisible kingdom out into the open. He would
much rather keep it secret. Second, because it shows the
supremacy and victory of God's kingdom over Satan's
kingdom. I deliberately began our examination of the
topic of spiritual warfare with this passage in Matthew
12 to emphasize and establish for you what the New
Testament clearly reveals: Two invisible spiritual kingdoms are at war with one another—the kingdom of God
and the kingdom of Satan.

CHAPTER TWO

A HIGHLY ORGANIZED SATANIC KINGDOM

For a brief description of the kingdom of Satan and its headquarters, we turn next to a statement Paul made that is absolutely key in our study of spiritual warfare:

> *For we do not wrestle against flesh and blood, but against principalities, against powers, against the rulers of the darkness of this age, against spiritual hosts of wickedness in the heavenly places.*
> (Ephesians 6:12)

To aid in our understanding of what Paul was saying about spiritual warfare, I would like to give you the amplified "Prince Version" of this verse. You may ask, "How is Derek Prince qualified to do that?" Well, I have studied Greek since I was ten years old, and I am qualified to teach it at the university level. That does not

necessarily mean I am always right, but I think I can offer an educated opinion. So, here is the "Prince Version"
of Ephesians 6:12:

> For our wrestling match is not against "persons
> with bodies"....

The phrase "persons with bodies" is borrowed from
The Living Bible, which describes the satanic forces as *"persons **without** bodies"* (Ephesians 6:12). I think this description provides some valuable insight. We are in a wrestling
match, but we are wrestling with beings who don't have
bodies. They are not human beings; they don't have *"flesh
and blood,"* as we do. Understanding this reality immediately causes us to adjust our thinking, because we are not
used to the concept of persons without bodies (although
there are multitudes of such "persons" in the universe).

Rulers with Authority

To continue in the "Prince Version":

> ...but against rulers with various areas and de-
> scending orders of authority.

We see from this passage that Satan's kingdom is
highly organized. There are rulers in his kingdom, each
with a particular area of responsibility. Under each of
those rulers are sub-rulers who are responsible for sub-
areas in that kingdom.

At first, it might seem as if Satan was very clever to devise such an organization, but this is not the case. Most scholars believe that before Satan fell, when he was still a mighty angel of God, he was in charge of one-third of the angels. He led those angels into rebellion against God, and, together, they were cast out of heaven. Satan then simply set up a rival kingdom, keeping the organizational structure that he and his angels had followed when they were a part of God's kingdom. So, Satan gets no credit for his extremely clever organization.

World Dominators of Darkness

I will recap the first part of Ephesians 6:12 in the "Prince Version" and then continue with it:

> For our wrestling match is not against "persons with bodies" but against rulers with various areas and descending orders of authority, against the world dominators of the present darkness....

I deliberately use the word *dominators* in translating from the Greek, because it is a powerful word. I also choose it because God never dominates anybody. Wherever you encounter domination, you can be sure that it is satanic. That is not how God rules people.

Satan's ambition, however, is to dominate the whole world. Do you understand that? He is not content with dominating a small portion of humanity. He is determined to rule the entire world through his kingdom of darkness.

For the most part, the people who are currently in Satan's kingdom don't realize where they really are, because it is a kingdom of darkness, and they can't "see" it. In contrast, the kingdom of God is the kingdom of light; therefore, those who are in His kingdom know where they are.

Spiritual Hosts of Wickedness

Here is the final phrase in the "Prince Version" of Ephesians 6:12:

> ...against spiritual hosts of wickedness in the heavenlies (heavenly places).

The word *hosts* is the Old English word for *army*. So, according to this Scripture, vast armies of satanic beings—persons without bodies—are arrayed in battle against us. It is important that we know this, isn't it? If we truly understand the nature and scope of the forces we are up against, it will adjust our perspective and transform our lives.

Understanding the "Heavenlies"

Let us next examine Paul's assertion that Satan's headquarters are in the heavenlies. There is a widespread misunderstanding among many church members who speak about Satan as if he is in hell. Hell is a place of confinement, below the surface of the earth, for wicked persons. Here is my comment on this misunderstanding: It would be nice if Satan *were* in hell, but he isn't. He is very much at large here on earth. He is extremely active. And his kingdom is in the heavenlies.

You may be thinking, *Didn't you just state that Satan and his angels were cast out of heaven?* Yes, that is true. However, the key to understanding the location of Satan's kingdom is to recognize that the Bible teaches that there are more heavens than the one we usually talk about. It is absolutely essential to understand this reality.

The first verse of the Bible says, "*In the beginning God created the heavens* [plural] *and the earth* [singular]" (Genesis 1:1). From the very beginning of the Bible, we have this revelation that there is more than one heaven.

Two passages in the New Testament clearly confirm this point. The first is 2 Corinthians 12:2–4, in which Paul was writing about people he knew who had enjoyed marvelous spiritual experiences. He mentioned one particular person who had been caught up from the earthly level into the heavenlies. Paul further said that he didn't know whether the person had this experience while in his body or outside of it.

*I know a man in Christ who fourteen years ago;
whether in the body I do not know, or whether out
of the body I do not know, God knows; such a one
was caught up to the **third heaven**. And I know
such a one; whether in the body or out of the body
I do not know, God knows; how he was caught
up into Paradise and heard inexpressible words,
which it is not lawful for a man to utter.*

(2 Corinthians 12:2–4)

Notice that Paul said this fellow Christian *"was
caught up to the third heaven."* He also said that he *"was
caught up into Paradise,"* which would seem to suggest
that *"Paradise"* is in the third heaven. Since, in the third
heaven, this man heard the words of God, the third
heaven (Paradise) would apparently be the dwelling
place of God.

I am a logician—I cannot escape from logic. And
one fact I am convinced of is this: If there is a third
heaven, there must be a first and a second. There never
has been a third of anything without a first and second.
So, this Scripture tells us that there are at least three
heavens. That is what I believe. (See also, for example,
Deuteronomy 10:14; Nehemiah 9:6.)

"All the Heavens"

One other Scripture that infers the existence of more than one heaven is Ephesians 4:10. Speaking of what happened to Jesus in His death and resurrection, Paul wrote:

> He who descended [into hell] is also the One who ascended far above all the heavens, that He might fill all things. (Ephesians 4:10)

Notice that Paul said, "[Jesus] *ascended far above* **all** *the heavens.*"

When I taught English as a second language in Africa, I discovered that there are certain aspects of English grammar that can be very confusing. You may have struggled with some of them yourself. One such pitfall is the use of the word *all*, because it cannot be used in certain situations.

For example, one day, a student came to me and said, "Please, sir, all my parents have come to see me." I said, "Well, I understand what you mean, but you're using the wrong word. You can't have more than two parents [though one might have two parents and two stepparents], and you can't use the word *all* for fewer than three people."

So, when Paul said that Jesus ascended *"above all the heavens,"* I understand that to mean there must have been (and still are) at least three heavens.

I am not claiming that my opinion is necessarily the only correct one, but I have concluded that the third heaven is the heaven of God's dwelling place. It is the holy heaven. Remember that God dwells above even heaven. The Bible states this fact in many places. (See, for example, 1 Kings 8:27; 2 Chronicles 2:6; 6:18; Psalm 8:1; Hebrews 7:26.) Therefore, I would suggest that the first heaven could be the visible heaven that we see— the sky above us, with the clouds. Then, there remains a second heaven—although it is never actually called that—which is somewhere between the visible heaven (sky) and the heaven of God's dwelling. I believe this second heaven is the "heavenlies," or *"heavenly places,"* where Satan's kingdom is located.

Maybe you will think I am naïve, but let me offer you the following theory. Over the course of my ministry, I have traveled a lot by plane. Once, on a flight from New Zealand to Singapore, Ruth and I were flying at an altitude of 39,000 feet, which is a long, long way up. At that height, I had the feeling that I was above Satan's kingdom. It felt like it was easier to pray. I didn't have to fight my way through opposition.

This may be completely my own subjective impression. But somewhere between God's heavenly domain and us is a hostile kingdom that opposes us and seeks to hinder our prayers. And that is why we sometimes have to push through enemy territory when we pray. It is not that we are praying out of the will of God, or that God is unwilling to hear us, but that we have to penetrate a hostile kingdom in the heavenlies in order to reach Him.

CHAPTER THREE

WAR IN THE HEAVENLIES

Rather than speculate on this matter of our battle in the heavenly realms, let's look at the scriptural account of Daniel's battle in prayer in chapters 10 through 12 of the book of Daniel. This account clearly illustrates the principle that we must penetrate Satan's hostile kingdom with our prayers. We will not examine the entire narrative, but, if you are interested, you would do well to read these three chapters for yourself.

Opposition by Satanic Angels

At the beginning of Daniel chapter 10, we see that Daniel had set aside a period of three weeks as a special time of prayer and fasting. Many Christians call the type of fast he went on a "Daniel fast." He did not give up eating entirely, but he ate a diet that consisted only of simple fruits and vegetables. He ate no meat and drank no wine.

In his fast, Daniel was mourning before God on behalf of his people Israel, who were captives of a Gentile empire. At the end of three weeks, a glorious angel, Gabriel, came to him with the answer to his prayers and a revelation from God (explained in Daniel 11 and 12) concerning the future of his people.

Let us read the angel's announcement.

Then [the angel Gabriel] *said to me, "Do not fear, Daniel, for from the first day that you set your heart to understand, and to humble yourself before your God, your words were heard; and I have come because of your words. But the prince of the kingdom of Persia withstood me twenty-one days; and behold, Michael, one of the chief princes, came to help me, for I had been left alone there with the kings of Persia."* (Daniel 10:12–13)

To paraphrase, the angel was saying, "The first day you began to pray, you were heard, and I was sent with the answer to your prayer. But it took me three weeks to get through to you, because somewhere between the throne of God and you, I was opposed by satanic angels. I had to force my way through those angels."

An Obstructing Kingdom

It is very clear that at the time of Daniel, the satanic kingdom was located someplace between God's throne and the earth. Again, this fact has not changed. It was there when Paul wrote Ephesians 6:12, which was at least thirty years after the death, resurrection, and ascension of Jesus. In other words, whatever the organizational structure of Satan's kingdom had been, it was not changed by the death, resurrection, and ascension of Jesus. Jesus ascended far above Satan's kingdom, but Satan's kingdom remained in place.

Later in the text, the angel Gabriel told Daniel, in effect, "I have come with the answer to your prayer. But when I leave, I am going to have to fight my way back through the same angels. Then, I am going to have to fight other satanic angels." (See Daniel 10:20.)

The angel said that while he was on his way to Daniel, the prince of the kingdom of Persia had withstood him for twenty-one days. So, for twenty-one days, these angels were battling in the heavenlies.

Gabriel also spoke about *"the kings of Persia."* In the language of the *New King James Bible*, the word *"prince"* denotes a supreme ruler. *"Kings"* were sub-rulers. These rulers were all concerned with the empire of Persia, which, at that time, was the largest and most powerful empire on earth, with 127 provinces. So, Satan had one "super angel" who was responsible to him for the entire kingdom of Persia. But this evil angel had authority over other angels who were responsible for various areas within the kingdom of Persia. Since there were major cities in the Persian Empire, there probably was one sub-angel over each major city in the empire.

Evil Spiritual Influences

For me, the concept of demonic entities ruling over cities is not a mere theory. I have seen in my own ministry how this principle works. As I have traveled from city to city and from place to place, I have learned that to be effective in ministry in a certain locality, I often must identify the particular satanic power that is at work in that city. And it is different from city to city.

To take this concept further, let me also point out that there were many different nationalities within the Persian Empire. My observation is that there is often a particular satanic king over a specific ethnic group. In the United States, which is made up of a variety of ethnic groups, it is my clear impression that different ethnic groups have different satanic powers over them. In dealing with those ethnic groups spiritually, it becomes important to identify the power that is over them.

For instance, there is a significant African-American population in America. I love these brothers and sisters.

I have an African-American daughter. But many of them are the descendants of people who were brought to America as slaves. My opinion is that if your ancestor was a slave, you may have been politically emancipated, but if you have never been spiritually emancipated, you will remain under a spirit of slavery. I have shared this concept with black Americans who have agreed that this may be why some black Christians can progress only so far, and then something seems to stop them.

Applying this principle more broadly, when Paul spoke in Romans 8 about a *"spirit of bondage,"* or slavery, he said that we *"did not receive the spirit of bondage again to fear"* (verse 15), but we received the Spirit of God, who makes us *"children of God"* (verse 16). If you look at the context, the kind of bondage he was talking about was religious legalism—people whose religion consisted of sets of rules: "Do this." "Don't do that." My observation is that many African-Americans battle with legalism; they struggle to know the real liberty of God's grace. The reason is that the spirit of slavery has not been fully dealt with, and it still has a measure of control over them. As a group, they have never been set free, spiritually.

In the same regard, another group in the United States I would mention is the Native Americans. For the most part, the United States is a country of liberty where almost anyone can thrive because of the nature of the economy and the culture. A person does not have to acquire an advanced educational degree in order to prosper. However, as a whole, the Native Americans have not prospered. Many of them live in poverty; and, spiritually, many of them are still in darkness. A number of them are powerful practitioners of witchcraft. It is a tragedy, but my impression is that until someone with spiritual vision understands the root problem of Native Americans and is prepared to engage in the spiritual warfare necessary to release them, they will remain in bondage.

I think that if you ponder what I am saying, you will begin to see the same general principle operating in various groups in nations across the globe as a manifestation of spiritual warfare.

Spiritual Principles from the Experience of Daniel

At the end of the tenth chapter of Daniel, we learn another key factor regarding this war in the heavenlies. In verse 20, the angel had essentially told Daniel, "When I leave you, I will have to fight again with the prince of the kingdom of Persia, and then I will have to fight with the prince of the kingdom of Greece." Why Persia and Greece? Because they were two of the four Gentile empires that dominated God's people Israel and their land, including the city of Jerusalem, during and after the captivity. Four successive Gentile empires dominated Israel: Babylon, Persia, Greece, and Rome. In Daniel's day, Persia was still the dominant empire, but the next one would be Greece.

The battle is always the most spiritually intense wherever the key issues of God's kingdom are focused. Wherever God is at work, you will find Satan at work, also. The enemy's name essentially means "the resistor." How true! He resists God's purposes and His people. (See, for example, Zechariah 3:1 KJV.) He can't help it—he is a slave of his own nature.

It is paramount that we carry out spiritual warfare so that God's purposes for His people will be fulfilled. Daniel is a marvelous example of someone who, by prayer and fasting, affected the history and destiny of his people.

As a brief review, let's read through various passages in Daniel 10, and then I will add some comments in relation to spiritual warfare.

> *In those days I, Daniel, was mourning three full weeks. I ate no pleasant food, no meat or wine came into my mouth, nor did I anoint myself at all, till three whole weeks were fulfilled.* (Daniel 10:2–3)

Notice that the period of three weeks is emphasized, after which the angel Gabriel came to him and made various statements—most notably, the ones we find in the following passage:

> *Do not fear, Daniel, for from the first day that you set your heart to understand, and to humble yourself before your God, your words were heard; and I have come because of your words. But the prince of the kingdom of Persia withstood me twenty-one days; and behold, Michael, one of the chief princes, came to help me, for I had been left alone there with the kings of Persia.* (Daniel 10:12–13)

The angel of God was opposed by the prince of the kingdom of Persia for twenty-one days. In the end, another of God's angels, the archangel Michael, had to come and join in the conflict. In a later chapter of Daniel, Michael is called *"the great prince who stands watch over the sons of your people [Israel]"* (Daniel 12:1). As a matter of biblical interpretation, you will find this information helpful: Wherever Michael is on the scene, Israel is center stage in human history. This is because he is the particular angel who has the job of looking after Israel. (And, believe me, that is a tough job.)

Gabriel later told Daniel,

> *Do you know why I have come to you? And now I must return to fight with the prince of Persia* [in other words, the battle isn't over yet]; *and when I have gone forth, indeed the prince of Greece will come.*
>
> (Daniel 10:20)

The angel indicated that Greece would be the next Gentile empire whose principality he would encounter in spiritual warfare. From this account, we understand that behind the history of those human empires, there were satanic forces at work that were the real explanations for what happened in them and with them. You cannot fully understand human history if you look only on the horizontal, human level. The forces that truly determine the destinies of nations and people are at work in the heavenlies.

Then, Gabriel said,

> *But I will tell you what is noted in the Scripture of Truth. (No one upholds me against these, except Michael your prince....)* (Daniel 10:21)

Once more, we see the reference to the vital role of the archangel Michael. Let us move on to the first verse of the next chapter, which is actually part of the same message:

...Also in the first year of Darius the Mede, I, even I, stood up to confirm and strengthen him.

(Daniel 11:1)

The above is a clear example of the intervention of angels in human history. Why did God's angel stand up for Darius? The answer is clear. God's people, Israel, had been captured and enslaved by the empire of Babylon, but Darius was the ruler of the Persian Empire who destroyed the Babylonian Empire and released God's people to return to their own land. This was God's purpose.

So, let us remember that behind all the human forces that are engaged on a horizontal plane, there is a vertical plane where angelic forces—both angels of God and angels of Satan—are at work. Human history is truly explained by the interplay of these forces.

Entrusted with Spiritual Power

Why are we, as Christians, significant to the process of spiritual warfare? Because God has given to us—and to us alone—the armaments by which we can intervene on behalf of those who are being attacked by Satan and his kingdom. Some governments have vast armies and weapons with which to confront other nations or resist their attacks, but only the Christian church has the "military hardware" to intervene in the spiritual realm in the heavenlies. As we have seen in Daniel's case, the one who wins in the heavenlies ultimately determines the course of history. So, the most significant action you can take for the sake of history is to be an intercessor. By so doing, you will pray through spiritual issues in the heavenlies that will determine the history of nations on earth. Again, the angelic battle in the book of Daniel, and Daniel's part in that battle through fasting and prayer, is a perfect example of this truth.

As I noted earlier, those who are citizens of God's kingdom are already involved in spiritual warfare. It is not optional for them. The only decision we can make is whether or not we will be a part of the kingdom of God through faith in Jesus Christ and submission to His lordship. If you are already a part of His kingdom, then you are at war with the kingdom of Satan. You simply need to recognize this reality, become spiritually equipped, and learn how to fight against Satan's kingdom—because, if you don't, you are going to be a casualty of spiritual warfare. In the next chapter, we will explore this matter of becoming spiritually equipped and learning to do battle.

CHAPTER FOUR

SEVEN WEAPONS
OF WARFARE

Turning now to Ephesians 6, we will find out how to be equipped for spiritual battle by examining the apostle Paul's admonition on this topic, beginning in verse 13. Paul started the verse with a *"therefore."* In many of my books, I have discussed the fact that when you see a "therefore" in Scripture, you need to determine what it is "there for." In this case, it is there because of verse 12, which we read in the previous chapter and which describes Satan's kingdom in the heavenlies, or *"heavenly places"*:

> *For we do not wrestle against flesh and blood, but against principalities, against powers, against the rulers of the darkness of this age, against spiritual hosts of wickedness in the heavenly places.*
>
> (Ephesians 6:12)

Now that we know what the *"therefore"* is there for, let us read the next verse:

> *Therefore take up the whole armor of God, that you may be able to withstand in the evil day, and having done all, to stand.*   (Ephesians 6:13)

This verse is saying that an evil day is coming. Like it or not, an evil day comes in the life of every one of us, and Paul said that we had better put on our armor in preparation for it. Whether or not we will stand will depend on whether or not we put on the necessary equipment.

Armor for Spiritual Warfare

In Ephesians 6:14–17, Paul listed the elements of spiritual armor that we need, providing a picture of this armor from the example of a Roman legionary of his day. We will briefly review the six main items of armor and then discuss a final, powerful weapon for defeating Satan.

"Stand therefore, having girded your waist with truth" (Ephesians 6:14). The spiritual belt we must wear around our waist is the belt of truth.

"Having put on the breastplate of righteousness" (verse 14). A breastplate covers the chest and protects the heart. Spiritually, the breastplate that protects us is righteousness—not the righteousness of human works but the righteousness of faith in Christ.

"*Having shod your feet with the preparation of the gospel of peace*" (Ephesians 6:15). This verse is a reference to sandals that protect your feet and enable you to march far and fast, which Roman legionnaires would often do. Our spiritual sandals are "*the preparation of the gospel of peace.*" What is one way in which we can be ready to carry the gospel to others? Peter wrote, "*Always be prepared to give an answer to everyone who asks you to give the reason for the hope that you have*" (1 Peter 3:15 NIV).

"*Above all, taking the shield of faith with which you will be able to quench all the fiery darts of the wicked one*" (Ephesians 6:16). In Roman warfare, soldiers used a large shield, shaped like a door, which protected every part of their bodies from the arrows of the enemy. Similarly, the "*shield of faith*" will protect us from the enemy's "*fiery darts.*"

"*Take the helmet of salvation*" (verse 17). The helmet protects your head. And what does your head represent? Your thought life. God knows that it is very important for us to protect our thoughts, so He has provided the helmet of salvation for us. First Thessalonians 5:8 says, "[Put on] *as a helmet the hope of salvation.*" Hope protects your mind. You must be an optimist. If you are a pessimist, your mind is open to the attacks of Satan. This is something I learned by experience. I was born and bred a pessimist, and I suffered agonies in my mind until I learned I had to change. I had to train myself to put on the helmet that would protect my mind.

"And take…the sword of the Spirit, which is the word of God" (Ephesians 6:17). This refers to the *spoken* Word of God.

So far, we have looked at six items of equipment. All of them are defensive, protective weapons except for the last one. The sword, or the spoken Word of God, is an offensive weapon—a weapon of attack. However, a sword extends only as far as the arm can reach, so let us now look at the seventh weapon:

"Praying always with all prayer and supplication in the Spirit" (Ephesians 6:18). We can reach out and assail Satan's kingdom in the heavenlies with the weapon of "all prayer" in the Spirit. This seventh piece of equipment for warfare is what I call "God's intercontinental ballistic missile."

Let us, then, review these seven pieces of equipment that we must use in spiritual warfare:

1. The belt of truth
2. The breastplate of righteousness
3. The sandals of the preparation of the gospel of peace
4. The shield of faith
5. The helmet of salvation
6. The sword of the Spirit
7. All prayer

PART II

DEFEATING THE "STRONG MAN"

CHAPTER FIVE

BINDING
THE STRONG MAN

In this chapter, we come to the very crux of the matter of spiritual warfare. Going back to our initial text in Matthew 12, I will show you one more verse that I hope will stimulate your thinking. Really, that is all I can do, but that is a lot. If the church would only start thinking, we could not be defeated. It has always impressed me that Martin Luther started the Protestant Reformation by pinning up ninety-five theses on the church door at Wittenberg. He couldn't pin up all the answers—he just got everyone to start thinking. When they started thinking, things changed. That is how important it is for us to learn to think.

A Key Insight for Warfare

In Matthew 12:29, Jesus gave a key insight regarding the warfare between the kingdom of God and the kingdom of Satan:

> *Or how can one enter a strong man's house and plunder his goods, unless he first binds the strong man? And then he will plunder his house.*
> (Matthew 12:29)

This insight is what I call the "principle of the strong man." Jesus gave us a picture of a house belonging to a strong man—a despot, a cruel ruler—who has slaves and all sorts of stolen goods in his house. He has total control of his household, and it is very difficult to get in for the purpose of setting his slaves free or regaining the plunder. If you do get in, the whole time you are trying to free the strong man's slaves or recover his plunder, you are trying to fight him off.

Do you see the situation you would face if you tried to defeat the strong man in this manner? You could end up mortally wounded. Jesus wisely pointed out that simply gaining entrance is not the logical way to approach a situation of this type. The logical way is to begin by binding the strong man. First, tie him up and put a gag in his mouth. Then, you can walk in and out at liberty, helping yourself to what you need to recover and setting his captives free.

This is a significant spiritual principle. If you want to be successful in any given situation, you must discover who or what the satanic "strong man" is over that situation. Then, once you have bound the strong man, you can do what needs to be done. But the principle is to first bind the strong man—then set his captives free and recover what was lost.

As I wrote previously, Satan's kingdom descends from level to level; it is overseen by angelic beings that have various areas of responsibility. As they descend in order, the lower ones oversee smaller territories. Generally speaking, you don't start your campaign of spiritual warfare at the top. You start where you are. You learn the principles of warfare, and you learn how to implement them over smaller territories. Then, you advance to the level where you are dealing with a strong man over a city or even over a nation.

Perhaps you are experiencing problems as you try to succeed in doing the will of God. You may not be seeing the spiritual breakthroughs you hope for in your family, your business, or your church. Somehow, things are not going the way you feel they ought to, and you are perplexed by what you are encountering. My suggestion is that, in all probability, there are strong men over the situations confronting you. Frankly, you will not be really successful until you first deal with the strong man.

Recognizing a Strong Man in Your Life

I recall an experience from my own life when I had to deal with a strong man. The situation involved my family, which had grown over the years from nine adopted daughters to about 120 members! Basically, we have been blessed with a very good family. We love one another, we have stuck together in all sorts of difficult situations, and we are still in contact with one another all across the world.

But a circumstance arose that made me aware of the presence of a strong man in our family. Let me first give you some background.

After my first wife, Lydia, died, and before I married Ruth, I was a widower for two and a half years. It was a tradition in our family that we would celebrate Christmas Eve together, and we had one of these family events planned for a particular Christmas. Since I had a large house at that time, we would meet in my home.

The day before that Christmas Eve, I was pondering the upcoming family time together. Although we have loved one another and enjoyed good relationships, when all the family was gathered together, I would always feel a certain tension—a certain pressure. I think it was partly due to various of my daughters hoping that I would take more interest in their children than in another daughter's children. I thought to myself, *There must be something behind this.*

I was lying on my back in bed at about eleven o'clock at night, and I said, "Lord, what is really behind this?" Immediately, a kind of gray mist appeared in my room, just below the level of the ceiling. I understood that God was showing me that this was the power that was making relationships difficult in my family. So, I asked God, "What is it?" And He said, "Self-righteousness."

I pondered that response for a while, and I thought about my first wife. Lydia was a wonderful Christian, but, like many devoted Christians, she was very concerned about doing the right thing. Although that concern is often well-motivated, it can be a step toward self-righteousness. Next, I thought about myself. I admitted, *It certainly fits me!* With the Lord's help, I saw that our family was to some degree under the influence of a spirit of self-righteousness because both my first wife and I had been open to it.

You see, in the family structure, the parents should be the spiritual umbrella protecting the children. But if there is a hole in the umbrella, the enemy can get through and cause problems. I decided that the first step I needed to take was to repent and renounce self-righteousness for myself. (You can't do much for other people if you have the problem yourself—and I did.) Then I said, "Lord, let that power of self-righteousness over our family be broken, in the name of Jesus." When we came together the next day, it was quite different from our past gatherings. What had pressured us during previous holidays simply was not there.

This is just one example of the presence of a strong man. You may be a Christian businessperson who has a sincere desire to use your finances and talents for the Lord. But, somehow, your business never really prospers the way it should. Just when you are on the brink of a breakthrough, success eludes you. I want to suggest that there may be a strong man over your business.

Whatever your specific situation, ask God to reveal the strong man to you, because He alone has the solution to your difficulty. As He reveals it, repent of any sin He shows you; then, bind the strong man and enter into the fullness of life and prosperity that God desires for you.

CHAPTER SIX

STRONG MEN
OVER NATIONS

Now that we understand on a personal level the basic premise of this key insight about binding the strong man, let's move to the next level, for the same principle of the strong man is true for nations.

Once, I was teaching on this subject at a meeting in New Zealand, and someone asked me, "What is the strong man over New Zealand?" At first, I said it was the business of their spiritual leaders to find out the answer to that question. But others kept asking me, and, at a certain point, the Lord showed me the answer. Finally, giving in to their persistence, I said, "If you truly want to know, I believe the strong man over New Zealand is indifference."

I want to state here that I love the people of New Zealand. They are a warm, friendly people. In a way, however, they don't take life seriously. Their attitude is, "It will all work out in the end." In fact, they have a saying, "She'll be right, Jack."

Incidentally, before I had given the answer to their question, a friend of mine, who is a well-known businessman in New Zealand, had come in late to the meeting and had taken a seat next to his daughter. At the very moment that I said I felt God had shown me the strong man, this man turned to his daughter and said, "It's indifference." I would have to say that for many years since the time of those meetings, New Zealand has basically been on the decline politically, socially, and spiritually. The main problem is indifference. Until the Christians of New Zealand come to grips with that problem, I don't believe they will truly be able to deal with their national situation.

Breaking the Chains

Not to pick on only the New Zealanders, I was faced with the issue of being asked to identify the strong man of a nation during meetings in Australia. I told the people, "If you want to know what I believe, the spiritual problem of Australia is rejection." I have learned to be careful how I speak concerning Australians, but I am speaking boldly here, and I am also speaking out of a great love for Australians.

As you may or may not know, Australia was founded as a penal colony. Prisoners were routinely given the opportunity to go there, and they were often forced to do so as a punishment. Consequently, it is common to find in the thinking of the Australian people a sense of being outcasts or rejects.

Once, when I was teaching on this topic in Australia, God gave the most beautiful prophecy to a New Zealand man who was attending the meetings. In the prophecy, God said He was going to heal Australia and that He had compassion for that nation. In fact, God called it "the nation born in chains." But the Lord said He was going to break those chains. I believe that prophecy; I believe there is a tremendous revival coming to Australia in the near future.

Fortunes Affecting Nations

What is the strong man over the United States? Of course, there are many forces affecting America, but I would say that, essentially, it is rebellion. You see, the United States was conceived in rebellion. I've noticed an amazing phenomenon: When we British refer to the history of America's nationhood, we talk about the American War of Independence. The Americans call it the American Revolution. Isn't that astonishing? Bear in mind, I am not criticizing those who revolted. If I had been a colonist in the days of George Washington, I would have done the same. But the fact of the matter is that the nation of the United States was conceived in rebellion.

The Scriptures tell us there is something that is closely connected with rebellion: *"Rebellion is as the sin of witchcraft"* (1 Samuel 15:23). So, the other strong power over the United States is witchcraft. These are just a few simple examples of how nations are influenced or controlled by strong men. I probably ought to end this discussion before I offend someone, but let's continue anyhow.

Identifying the Strong Man

What is the problem with the British? The British are complicated people. It is difficult to express their problems with just one word. However, let me give it a try. What I tell people is that if you want to know the difference between the Americans and the British—and I am both—the Americans will tell you how good they are, but the British expect you to know without being told!

I don't have any doubt that the strong man over Britain is pride. Again, I don't say this to be critical. I am simply laying out the truth as I see it, all in the context of a great love for the nations I have mentioned.

My aim is to diagnose the main issue that is the strong man in order to help us to deal with it effectively. The point is, whether in regard to a person or a nation, our first step is to identify the strong man in the situation and then begin the process of binding him in prayer.

CHAPTER SEVEN

POWERFUL WEAPONS

As we come to the conclusion of part II, let's examine some additional powerful weapons that we can utilize in defeating the strong man.

"Binding" and "Loosing"

First of all, we are to "bind" and "loose" spiritual forces through prayer. Jesus gave us these important revelations:

> Assuredly, I say to you, whatever you bind on earth will be bound in heaven, and whatever you loose on earth will be loosed in heaven.
>
> (Matthew 18:18)

What a tremendous statement! The original Greek may be translated as follows, with my emphasis: "Whatever you bind on earth *will be having been bound* in heaven." So, the moment you bind it on earth, it is bound in heaven. Do you realize the significance of that truth?

We have the power to intervene in the heavenly realm. If we meet the conditions on earth, we can bind something on earth that will be bound in heaven. Likewise, we can loose something on earth that will be loosed in heaven.

Therefore, if we identify a group of people—a family, a community, or even a nation—that is bound by certain spiritual forces, we can take action to loose those forces and set the people free. Again, to paraphrase from the original Greek, "Whatever you loose on earth *will be having been loosed* in heaven." Jesus clearly stated that if you loose the forces on earth, they will be loosed in heaven. In a way, we are not waiting for God to do something about various situations—God is waiting for us. An attitude of passivity is not pleasing to God.

Agreement

Next, Jesus attached a condition that we must be aware of:

> *Again I say to you that if two of you agree on earth concerning anything that they ask, it will be done for them by My Father in heaven.* (Matthew 18:19)

In the Greek, the word translated as *"agree"* means "to symphonize or harmonize." Jesus connected to the promise of binding and loosing the condition of being able to harmonize. If two people harmonize in prayer and ask for something, they will receive it. However, it is not that easy to harmonize.

I believe the reason for this promise is that the only way we can harmonize is by the Holy Spirit. If we harmonize by the Spirit, we will be in agreement with what God wants. So, if a husband and wife can agree, they will receive whatever they pray for. But, again, agreement is a tremendous challenge, especially for Christian couples. It is simply not very easy for husbands and wives to harmonize in prayer.

It is pretty easy to be *almost* in harmony. However, musically speaking, to be almost in harmony is to be excruciatingly dissonant. You will find that the devil will fight your harmonizing in every way he can, because he is afraid of the power of agreement in prayer.

Thanksgiving

Another tremendous weapon is the giving of thanks to God. Let me point out a very interesting outworking of thanksgiving in the ministry of Jesus. In John 6, we find the account of Jesus feeding the five thousand:

And Jesus took the loaves, and when He had given thanks He distributed them to the disciples, and the disciples to those sitting down; and likewise of the fish, as much as they wanted. (John 6:11)

When reading this verse, have you ever noticed that Jesus did not pray? All He did was give thanks. And the giving of thanks over five loaves and two fishes made this small amount of food sufficient to feed five thousand people!

Note what the Scriptures say a little further on:

However, other boats came from Tiberias, near the place where they ate bread after the Lord had given thanks. (John 6:23)

What released the miracle? Again, it was the act (and the attitude) of giving thanks.

Praise

Praising God is an additional spiritual weapon. The Word of God says,

From the lips of children and infants you have ordained praise ["strength" KJV, NKJV] because of your enemies, to silence the foe and the avenger.
(Psalm 8:2 NIV)

"*The foe and the avenger*" is Satan. He needs to be silenced because he is constantly accusing you and me before the throne of God. (See, for example, Revelation 12:10.) God Himself does not silence Satan, because He has given us the weapons to do so.

In Acts 16, we read that Paul and Silas were thrown into prison. They were placed in the maximum security section of the jail, where they were chained and had their feet fastened in stocks. At midnight, as they were praying and praising God, something happened. God sent an earthquake that released the whole prison contingent—it opened all the prison doors and loosed everyone's chains. (See Acts 16:19–26.) What released that earthquake? Praise!

Proclamation

The power of proclamation is the one weapon the church needs to major in these days. When God called Moses to go to Egypt and deliver the Israelites out of slavery, Moses said, in effect, "But God, I don't have anything." In response, God asked him, "*What is that in your hand?*" (Exodus 4:2). To paraphrase, Moses replied, "That is just my shepherd's rod." God said, "Throw it down on the ground!" When Moses did what God commanded, his rod became a snake, and he ran away from his own rod. He failed to realize the power he had in his own hand. God then said to Moses, "All you need to deliver Israel is that one rod. Go, and use it." (See Exodus 3:1–4:17.) And with that one rod, Moses wrested the rule of Egypt out of the hand of Pharaoh, bringing about the release of the Israelites on God's behalf. (See Exodus 5–16.)

You may be saying, "I don't have anything," but God is saying, "What do you have in your hand?" For most of us, all we have in our hand is a Bible. That is all you need. Just take that "rod" and stretch it out. You stretch out the rod by making proclamations of what the Bible says concerning you.

I encourage you never to let a day pass without making a proclamation from the Scriptures. Therefore, let's close this chapter by taking a bold step and making Deuteronomy 33:25–27 (NIV) our proclamation:

> The bolts of [our] gates will be iron and bronze, and [our] strength will equal [our] days. There is no one like the God of Jeshurun, who rides on the heavens to help [us] and on the clouds in his majesty. The eternal God is [our] refuge, and underneath are the everlasting arms. He will drive out [our] enemy before [us], saying, "Destroy him!"

That settles it!

If you make proclamations like that on a daily basis, you should see the removal of the strong man over your life, your family, your church, and even your business. Add to proclamation the weapons of warfare we examined in chapter 4, as well as the other weapons we covered in this chapter—binding and loosing, agreement, thanksgiving, and praise—and you should be well on your way to victory in the realm of spiritual warfare.

In part III of this book, we will take these principles further as we deal with the role of the church in the nation—specifically, the responsibility we Christians carry for removing the "high places" and pulling down strongholds.

TEARING DOWN
THE "HIGH PLACES"

CHAPTER EIGHT

THE OFFENSE OF HIGH PLACES

In our examination of the concept of "high places," I want to issue a challenge to you right from the start: I ask you to be fully engaged in what we are about to cover. To this purpose, let's look at an incident from the life of Jesus.

Throughout the course of His ministry, Jesus was regularly confronted by the religious leaders of His day, who were often intent upon trapping Him in an attempt to discredit Him in word or deed. During one such conflict, one of the scribes, impressed by Jesus' wisdom, stepped forward and asked, "Teacher, which is the greatest of all the commandments?" (See Mark 12:28.)

What was Jesus' answer? *"You shall love the LORD your God* [note carefully what follows:] *with all your heart, with all your soul, with all your mind, and with all your strength"* (Mark 12:30).

We must not forget that the mind—as well as the heart, soul, and strength—is vital to loving the Lord. I stress this point because of my experiences during my pilgrimage through various stages of Christianity, in which I have ministered to groups from numerous denominations. Many of these groups believed that when they came to a meeting, they could safely leave their minds in their cars in the parking lot, because they would not need them in church.

As I stressed earlier, Christians must learn to think if they are to defeat Satan. And you are going to need your mind in order to fully grasp the importance of this topic of removing the high places.

A Repeated Warning!

The idea for our emphasis in this chapter first came to me some years ago, at a time when I was studying the books of 1 and 2 Kings. A recurring statement in those books captured my attention: *"But the high places were not removed." "Nevertheless the high places were not taken away."* (See, for example, 1 Kings 15:14; 22:43; 2 Kings 12:3; 14:4; 15:4; 15:35.)

I said to myself, *If God has taken the trouble to have that statement repeated so many times in His Word, there must be some importance to it.* I made a mental note that there was something about "high places" that I needed to look into. As happens at times, I put the note in my mental "pending file" and just left it there.

Rather to my surprise, about five years later, as I was preparing for a speaking engagement, the Lord reminded me about that mental note. I felt He had shown me that it was time to go into this matter of high places and share it with His people. Soon afterward, I spoke on the topic at a university, and a great number of students attended the lecture. They came expecting to engage their minds fully in order to lay the foundation for success in life. They understood that to be a successful Christian, you have to use your mind.

So, as we study the issue of "high places," be prepared to make a mental effort. You will need to put yourself back in time—into a period of history that is very remote and into a culture that is very different from ours. As you do, you will readily see why God wants us to understand the Old Testament problem of "high places." It is because this issue is as significant for the church today as it was for Israel at the time when God was emphatically warning His people about it.

CHAPTER NINE

THE PLACE OF TRUE WORSHIP

When Israel entered the land that God had promised them, it was occupied by the Canaanites. These Canaanites were wicked people, and the essence of their wickedness was their worship of idols. I believe idolatry is the greatest of all sins and the most disastrous in its consequences. To commit idolatry is to break the first commandment: *"You shall have no other gods before Me"* (Exodus 20:3).

In the Canaanite culture, idol worship was marked by abominable practices, including the sacrifice of infant children in ovens to a god named Molech. The Canaanites normally carried out those practices on what were called "high places."

High places were mountains or hills that stood about the surrounding country. In most cases, tall, impressive trees grew on the hills. That is why you will find phrases like this one repeated again and again in the historical and prophetic books of the Old Testament: *"on the high mountains and on the hills and under every green tree"* (Deuteronomy 12:2). As we will see, those phrases are always associated with the abomination of idolatry.

Ignoring God's Warning

The core purpose of a high place was to be a location for worshipping deities. God had clearly warned the children of Israel about the high places before they went into the Promised Land. We see that clear warning in the book of Deuteronomy, where God told them, in effect, "When you go into the land, I don't want you doing what the Canaanites have done. I have a different plan for you. I am appointing one place in a certain city where you can worship Me, and where you can offer your sacrifices. I don't want you to worship Me in any other place."

God's warning to Israel about not using the high places was clear and emphatic. Here is a portion of what He said to the Israelites through Moses:

These are the statutes and judgments which you shall be careful to observe in the land which the

LORD God of your fathers is giving you to possess, all the days that you live on the earth. You shall utterly destroy all the places where the nations which you shall dispossess served their gods, on the high mountains and on the hills and under every green tree. And you shall destroy their altars, break their sacred pillars, and burn their wooden images with fire; you shall cut down the carved images of their gods and destroy their names from that place. You shall not worship the LORD your God with such things. But you shall seek the place where the LORD your God chooses, out of all your tribes, to put His name for His dwelling place; and there you shall go. There you shall take your burnt offerings, your sacrifices, your tithes, the heave offerings of your hand, your vowed offerings, your freewill offerings, and the firstborn of your herds and flocks.

(Deuteronomy 12:1–6)

Unmistakably, God was saying, "I'm going to choose one place where I will put My name and where I will have My dwelling. That will be the only place I will permit you to offer sacrifices and worship to Me."

The Place Where God's Name Abides

It would be some time before it became clear that Jerusalem was the place of God's sanctuary referred to in the above verses. Many people don't realize it, but this is why the Jews worship at the Western Wall of that particular place today. That is as near as they can come to the site, because it is now occupied by a Muslim mosque.

The Jews are perfectly clear in their conviction that there is no other location where they can offer sacrifice. Consequently, in their thinking, their whole future centers on regaining possession of that place—because until they do, they cannot really offer sacrifice. While you may find it hard to understand this mind-set, it is a very controversial issue in the Middle East. It is the focal point of the clash between Muslims and Jews, and it demonstrates to us that God's Word is still remarkably relevant today.

Returning to our passage, we read:

> *Then there will be the place where the LORD your God chooses to make His name abide. There you shall bring all that I command you: your burnt offerings, your sacrifices, your tithes, the heave offerings of your hand, and all your choice offerings which you vow to the LORD.*

> (Deuteronomy 12:11)

From these verses, we understand that God intended for there to be one place where He would put His name; and, once that location was established, the children of Israel were not to worship in any other place.

CHAPTER TEN

A SOURCE OF CONTINUAL CONFLICT

The history of Israel, from the establishment of the monarchy until the Babylonian captivity, is marked by continual conflict regarding the high places. The Israelites constantly struggled between obeying God by worshipping Him in the appointed place and disobeying Him by going back to the high places.

In 1 Kings 3, we get an interesting glimpse of this struggle. Although what we are examining took place in the history of Israel three thousand years ago, it has a very important application for you and me today. Let us begin to lay the basis for this application by reading the following passage:

> *Now Solomon made a treaty with Pharaoh king of Egypt, and married Pharaoh's daughter; then*

> *he brought her to the City of David until he had*
> *finished building his own house, and the house*
> *of the LORD, and the wall all around Jerusalem.*
> *Meanwhile the people sacrificed at the high places,*
> *because there was no house built for the name of*
> *the LORD until those days.* (1 Kings 3:1–2)

At this point, the people were sacrificing to the Lord. They were not sacrificing to idols. Yet they were sacrificing on the high places because the temple in Jerusalem, where God was going to put His name, was not yet completed.

Solomon's Weakness

Continuing in the passage from 1 Kings 3, we find a comparison between Solomon and David that speaks volumes.

> *And Solomon loved the LORD, walking in the stat-*
> *utes of his father David, except that he sacrificed*
> *and burned incense at the high places.*
> (1 Kings 3:3)

Here we see a significant difference between David and Solomon. David never worshipped at the high places. Solomon did. In a certain sense, that was the weakness that ultimately led to Solomon's downfall.

By contrast, let's look at an account in 2 Chronicles of something that took place before the temple was built, when Solomon was made king:

> Then Solomon, and all the assembly with him, went to the high place that was at Gibeon; for the tabernacle of meeting with God was there, which Moses the servant of the LORD had made in the wilderness.
> (2 Chronicles 1:3)

Notice that, in the very next verse, the Bible makes the very important distinction that Gibeon was not Jerusalem.

> But David had brought up the ark of God from Kirjath Jearim to the place David had prepared for it, for he had pitched a tent for it at Jerusalem.
> (2 Chronicles 1:4)

David had grasped the fact that God wanted Jerusalem to be the place of worship. David did not take the ark to Gibeon. He took it to the place he had prepared for it in Jerusalem.

Second Samuel describes David bringing the ark back to Israel after it had been recovered from the Philistines.

> So David and all the house of Israel brought up the ark of the LORD with shouting and with the sound of the trumpet. Now as the ark of the LORD came into the City of David, Michal, Saul's daughter,

> looked through a window and saw King David
> leaping and whirling before the LORD; and she
> despised him in her heart. [That was a mis-
> take on her part!] So they brought the ark of the
> LORD, and set it in its place in the midst of the
> tabernacle that David had erected for it [not the
> tabernacle of Moses]. Then David offered burnt
> offerings and peace offerings before the LORD.
> (2 Samuel 6:15–17)

Again, David understood the absolute importance
of worshipping in the place of the Lord's appointment—
Jerusalem, the "City of David." Though the tabernacle of
Moses was in Gibeon, and the temple had not yet been
built, David, being a man after God's own heart (see
1 Samuel 13:14; Acts 13:22), said, "This place, Jerusalem,
is the place where I am going to worship God."

Please stay mentally engaged in the issues we are
covering here, because they will have specific application
to our lives in the sections just ahead.

Missing the Target

Certainly, David's son Solomon followed him in
much of what he had done. But Solomon departed from
David in this one respect—until the temple was built, he
worshiped in a high place.

You will find that later on in Solomon's experience, this seemingly minor discrepancy became a disease. When you begin to depart a little from God's path, you will get farther and farther away from His ways the longer you go in that direction. In 1 Kings 11, we read how this process unfolded in Solomon's life:

> *Then Solomon built a high place for Chemosh the abomination of Moab, on the hill that is east of Jerusalem* [the Mount of Olives], *and for Molech the abomination of the people of Ammon.*
>
> (1 Kings 11:7)

First Kings 11:8 tells us that Solomon built a high place for each of his foreign wives to worship her pagan idols. Then, we read in the next two verses:

> *So the LORD became angry with Solomon, because his heart had turned from the LORD God of Israel, who had appeared to him twice, and had commanded him concerning this thing, that he should not go after other gods; but he did not keep what the LORD had commanded.* (1 Kings 11:9–10)

I trust you can see by now that this issue of high places is of tremendous importance in the sight of God. In chapter 11, we will cover more of the history of Israel's kings in relation to this issue, and then we will make some striking applications.

CHAPTER ELEVEN

A TRAGIC PATTERN

If you were to read through the entire history of the kings of Israel, you would find it to be a very wearisome repetition in which the nation kept going back to the wrong practices of the Canaanites. Yet, as we briefly examine the history of Israel's repeatedly giving in to false spiritual practices, let's keep in mind one burning question: Is our nation falling prey to the same tendency?

After Solomon's reign, the kingdom of Israel became a divided monarchy: Jeroboam ruled the northern kingdom, called Israel, while Rehoboam ruled the southern kingdom, called Judah. Both kings returned to the high places. In 1 Kings 12, we read about King Jeroboam's disobedience:

> [Jeroboam] *made shrines on the high places, and made priests from every class of people, who were not of the sons of Levi.* (1 Kings 12:31)

Jeroboam offered sacrifices on the high places and appointed false priests. That is the historical record.

First Kings 14 tells us that Rehoboam, who was Solomon's son, also worshipped at the high places:

> *And Rehoboam the son of Solomon reigned in Judah....Now Judah did evil in the sight of the* LORD, *and they provoked Him to jealousy with their sins which they committed, more than all that their fathers had done. For they also built for them-selves high places, sacred pillars, and wooden im-ages on every high hill and under every green tree.* (1 Kings 14:21–23)

Are you beginning to see the repeated refrain? The same pattern continues on and on, over and over.

"He Did What Was Right, But..."

God raised up a son to Rehoboam, named Asa, who was a righteous king. We read about him in the next chapter of 1 Kings.

> *In the twentieth year of Jeroboam king of Israel,*
> *Asa became king over Judah....Asa did what was*
> *right in the eyes of the LORD, as did his father*
> *David. And he banished the perverted persons*
> *from the land, and removed all the idols that his*
> *fathers had made.*   (1 Kings 15:9, 11–12)

But King Asa also missed the mark, as we read in verse 14: "*But the high places were not removed.*"

Asa made good progress with his reforms, but he couldn't complete them. He restored the worship of the true God, but he did not restore the right place of worship. Instead, he kept the high places.

Here again is essentially the refrain that runs through 1 and 2 Kings: "He did what was right in the eyes of the Lord, but the high places were not taken away." The next king after Asa was Jehoshaphat, and he, also, was a righteous king. He put away all idolatry, and he restored the true worship of Jehovah—but the high places were not taken away.

After Jehoshaphat came Amaziah, who also restored the true worship of Jehovah—but the high places were not taken away.

Jehoash became king when he was seven years old. He did what was right in the sight of the Lord—but the high places were not taken away.

After Jehoash came Azariah (also called Uzziah). He maintained the true worship of Jehovah—but the high places were not taken away.

After Azariah came Jotham, who also maintained the true worship of Jehovah—but the high places were not taken away.

Under the leadership of these kings, Israel had a mixture of true and false. One after another, those six kings initiated good reforms, but they went only so far. They banished idolatry, but they didn't banish the use of the places where the false gods and idols had been worshipped. And God records of every one of them that he did not take away the high places. As I mentioned previously, they were worshipping the true God, unlike those who had gone into idolatry. But they were worshipping the true God in geographical areas that had been consecrated to the worship of idols. What these kings accomplished was a kind of partial reform. They got rid of the idols, but they did not get rid of the false basis of worship.

After these six kings—Asa, Jehoshaphat, Jehoash, Amaziah, Azariah, and Jotham—came Ahaz, who bypassed partial reform and went back to abject idolatry. The Bible describes Ahaz as a singularly wicked king.

But [Ahaz] walked in the way of the kings of Israel; indeed he made his son pass through the fire [he

offered his son as a living sacrifice in an oven],
*according to the abominations of the nations whom
the LORD had cast out from before the children of
Israel. And he sacrificed and burned incense on
the high places, on the hills, and under every green
tree.* (2 Kings 16:3–4)

God's Measurement

The repetition of Israel's turning away from God,
and then not fully obeying Him when they did return
to Him, may be a little wearisome. But it is pounding
into our minds a recognition of the truth. Many truths
in the Bible are presented in simple, categorical statements. Yet sometimes, truth in the Bible is revealed in
patterns that are continuously repeated, and God leads
us to discover an important lesson from these patterns.

The northern kingdom of Israel eventually went
into captivity under the Assyrians. Chapter 17 of
2 Kings sums up all the sins that caused the northern
kingdom to go into exile. Let's read a portion of what the
Bible says about this situation:

Also the children of Israel [the northern king-
dom] *secretly did against the LORD their God
things that were not right, and they built for themselves high places in all their cities, from watchtower*

*to fortified city. They set up for themselves sacred
pillars and wooden images on every high hill and
under every green tree. There they burned incense
on all the high places, like the nations whom the
LORD had carried away before them; and they did
wicked things to provoke the LORD to anger.*

(2 Kings 17:9–11)

We can plainly see that a major issue of contention
between God and His people was the high places. In
fact, the life and reign of every king who ruled over His
people was measured in regard to what he did about the
high places.

Two Righteous Kings

Quite near the end of the history of Judah, the
southern kingdom, there were two kings who did what
God had been waiting for. Hezekiah and Josiah were
outstandingly righteous kings.

*And [Hezekiah] did what was right in the sight
of the LORD, according to all that his father David
had done.*   (2 Kings 18:3)

You will remember that David never went to the
high places. Yet all of his descendants had failed to follow his example—up to this point.

[Hezekiah] **removed the high places** and broke the sacred pillars, cut down the wooden image and broke in pieces the bronze serpent that Moses had made; for until those days the children of Israel burned incense to it, and called it Nehushtan. He trusted in the LORD God of Israel, so that after him was none like him among all the kings of Judah, nor who were before him.

(2 Kings 18:4–5)

What was the distinguishing feature of Hezekiah's reign? What earned him that particular commendation in Scripture? He thoroughly dealt with the high places.

Surprisingly, Hezekiah experienced a disaster in regard to his son Manasseh, who was perhaps the most wicked of all the kings of Judah. You might remember, incidentally, that Hezekiah had his own life miraculously prolonged fifteen years in answer to his prayer when he was deathly ill. (See 2 Kings 20:1–11.) When he died, his son Manasseh was twelve years old. So, Manasseh was born during those extra fifteen years. If Hezekiah had not lived that extra time, he would not have produced wicked Manasseh. That fact teaches us that if God gives us extra time, we had better be careful what we do with it. I sometimes wonder if Hezekiah, in hindsight, would have changed his mind. Had he been given the choice again, knowing what Manasseh would do, would he have asked for those fifteen years?

Let's look very briefly at what the Bible says about Manasseh:

> He rebuilt the high places which Hezekiah his father had destroyed; he raised up altars for Baal, and made a wooden image, as Ahab king of Israel had done; and he worshipped all the host of heaven and served them.　　(2 Kings 21:3)

The Bible states that, of all the kings of Judah, there was none as wicked as Manasseh. (See 2 Kings 21:2–16.) And yet, amazingly enough, in 2 Chronicles 33:10–19, we learn that he repented. And God pardoned him! There it is in history. He was the most wicked king, and yet repentance brought him pardon from God.

Let us now review the life of the second righteous king. King Josiah did what God wanted:

> Then [Josiah] removed the idolatrous priests whom the kings of Judah had ordained to burn incense on the high places in the cities of Judah....He brought all the priests from the cities of Judah, and defiled the high places where the priests had burned incense.... Then the king defiled the high places that were east of Jerusalem.　　(2 Kings 23:5, 8, 13)

Obviously, Josiah conducted a war against the high places. Continuing with verse 15, we read:

> *Moreover the altar that was at Bethel, and the high place which Jeroboam the son of Nebat, who made Israel sin, had made, both that altar and the high place he broke down; and he burned the high place and crushed it to powder, and burned the wooden image.* (2 Kings 23:15)

Do you see what distinguished Josiah, setting him apart as a particularly righteous king? He dealt with the high places. Even though the majority of the kings of Judah worshipped the true God, they did not do away with the idolatrous sites of worship. They permitted the people to worship the true God—but on the wrong basis and in the wrong places.

CHAPTER TWELVE

WHAT ABOUT US?

We have spent a lot of time looking at the history of Israel. But the key question is whether that history has anything to say to you and me as Christians today. I believe it does. And I believe this is why, after several years, God brought the subject of the high places out of my mental "pending file."

We must ask ourselves the following questions:

+ What is the basis on which we can worship the true God acceptably?

+ What is the basis on which we are to come to Him?

+ What is the true place of worship?

Are we going to be like those Israelites who went to idolatrous places to worship, even if we are committed to worshipping the true God? Or, are we going to be like David, Hezekiah, and Josiah, who spurned the high places and worshipped God only on the basis that He had decreed?

Worship That Is Acceptable to God

The ultimate question is this: What is the basis of true worship that is acceptable to God, according to the New Testament? In other words, under the new covenant, what corresponds to worshipping God in His appointed place—the place where He has "made His name abide"? I believe the answer is found in a single verse: Matthew 18:20.

Some of what I am about to say may strike you as controversial. (I never aim to be controversial, but somehow I never seem to escape from it.) We will read Matthew 18:20 from the *New King James Version*, and then I will give you the "Prince Version" of this verse. A woman once asked me if the "Prince Version" was in print. The answer is no. This is my own impromptu translation. As I mentioned, I started learning the Greek language when I was ten years old; I studied it continuously for fifteen years, and I am qualified to teach it at the university level. That doesn't mean I am always correct, but, again, I think it gives me the right to express my opinion on how a passage can be interpreted.

LED TOGETHER, INTO HIS NAME

In the *New King James Version* we read:

For where two or three are gathered together in My name, I am there in the midst of them.

(Matthew 18:20)

The Greek word translated *"gathered together"* is *sunago*, and its literal meaning is "to be led together." One of the root words of *sunago* is the verb *ago*, which is the standard Greek word for "to lead," or "to drive."

So, a more literal translation of the first part of Matthew 18:20 would be, "As many as are led by the Spirit of God…," or "Where two or three have been led together…." It is in the perfect tense. Also, the preposition is not "in" but "into": "Where they have been led *into* My name, I am there in the midst."

The Lord never promised to meet Israel on a high hill, or on the high places. But He did say, in effect, "If you come to the place where I have put My name, I will be there."

This simple text holds many significant implications. If we say, "Where two or three have been led together," that raises the question, "Who led them?"

The answer is very clear and is found in Romans:

*For as many as are [regularly] led by the Spirit of
God, these are sons of God.*   (Romans 8:14)

That is a key Scripture. How do you become a child
of God? By being born again by the Spirit of God. But
to grow to be a mature son or daughter, you have to be
regularly led by the Spirit of God.

LED BY THE SPIRIT

Millions of Christians who have been born again
have no idea of how to be led by the Holy Spirit. As a result, they remain perpetual infants. They never mature.
I have preached to large audiences of people, of whom
the majority were saved and filled with the Holy Spirit.
Often, I have asked them, "How many of you have heard
a sermon on how to be born again?" Nearly everybody
would raise their hands. Then, I would ask, "How many
have heard a sermon on how to be regularly led by the
Spirit of God?" The average response to that question
has been less than 10 percent.

That poor response points out one of the great, fun-
damental problems of the charismatic renewal. Many
people talk about the Holy Spirit, but hardly anyone
knows how to be led by the Holy Spirit. As a result,
without realizing it, we go back to our little rituals and
our little sets of rules. By doing so, in essence, we are

going back to the high places (although, again, we may not realize it). Romans 8:14 tells us the only pathway to maturity: *"As many as are* [regularly] *led by the Spirit of God, these are sons* [not children, but mature sons] *of God."*

"As many as have been led together...." By whom? *"By the Spirit of God."* Do you realize the ramifications of that truth? You cannot leave the Spirit of God out of your life and still get results.

For example, do you think the Lord attends every meeting of the board of deacons in our churches? I think He is too much of a gentleman to be at some of those meetings. The Lord has never promised to attend every meeting of the boards of deacons, because many of those meetings are not led by the Spirit of God. But, the Lord states, "Where two or three have been led together by My Spirit...." Where did God say He would meet us? Where we have gathered together by the leading of the Spirit *into* the name of Jesus.

Although the church has had multitudinous reforms over the centuries, most of them, like the reforms of the kings of Judah, never dealt with the "high places," or the basis of our meeting together. Historically, we have had various other premises upon which we have met together. In my understanding, these are high places, yet they have not been recognized or addressed.

God does not authorize any other basis for Christians to come together but the basis of being led by the Holy Spirit into the name of Jesus. Any other place—any other basis—is a "high place."

CHAPTER THIRTEEN

THREE MODERN
HIGH PLACES

In this chapter, we will explore three false bases for meeting together that have become "high places" for the church: (1) the basis of nationality, (2) the basis of a particular doctrine, and (3) the basis of loyalty to a specific human leader.

1. The Basis of Nationality

First, our churches often meet on the basis of nationality. For example, Great Britain has a state church, the Church of England, in which I grew up. Likewise, all the Scandinavian nations—Denmark, Sweden, Norway, and Finland—have state churches. There is no basis in Scripture for this practice. There is nothing in the New Testament that authorizes a church to be based on nationality.

In the Lord Jesus Christ, there is no nationality. As Paul wrote, there is neither Greek nor Jew, citizen nor barbarian. (See Colossians 3:11.) Therefore, it is not biblical to talk about, for example, the English church, the Swedish church, or the African church. We can talk about the church *in* Great Britain, Sweden, or Africa, but that has a totally different meaning. It refers to the members of the body of Christ in those nations. In the New Testament, there are references to the church at Corinth, the church at Ephesus, the church at Thessalonica, and the church at Laodicea, to name a few. But neither Paul nor any of the other New Testament writers specified a church based on its belonging to a certain nation.

To clarify this concept further, you may correctly refer to the church in America, but any given congregation in the United States could be made up of believers who come from various nations of the world. Each nationality does not need to have a special church for itself. The only reason why believers of a particular national or ethnic background might need a special church is if they all speak a language that is not spoken by others in their community. But that is a matter of communication and not a basis for meeting together.

2. The Basis of a Particular Doctrine

Another erroneous basis upon which people meet together in church is what I call the "doctrinal" basis. They meet together because they are Baptists, Pentecostals, or any other denomination or affiliation. One such group of people might believe particularly in baptism by immersion, and another might believe especially in the baptism with the Holy Spirit; as a result, that specific doctrine becomes the basis on which they come together. However, meeting solely on the ground of a particular doctrinal basis is not authorized by Scripture.

I believe that God has been attempting, through notable activity of His Holy Spirit, to bring doctrinal unity to the body of Christ. How far we have cooperated with His attempts is questionable. Paul never wrote to specific denominational groups—"to the Baptist church in Corinth," or "to the Pentecostal church in Corinth." Suppose Paul wrote to "the church" in your city? To which church would his letter be delivered?

3. The Basis of Loyalty to a Specific Human Leader

Some obvious examples of people meeting together on this basis are specific denominations that have been built on the teachings and example of prominent leaders in church history, such as Martin Luther or John Wesley. I thank the Lord for great men of God. However, the New Testament does not authorize believers to meet on the basis of association with a human leader.

In fact, Paul set aside this idea: *"Each of you says, 'I am of Paul,' or 'I am of Apollos,' or 'I am of Cephas,' or 'I am of Christ.' Is Christ divided? Was Paul crucified for you? Or were you baptized in the name of Paul?"* (1 Corinthians 1:12–13). Paul's implication is that there is only one name of importance, and that is the name of Jesus Christ.

A Call for a New Reformation

Do you see the connection between the practices of the kings of Judah in the Old Testament and the practices of the church in the twenty-first century? Have we in the modern church created our own "high places" in which to worship God—places that He Himself has not chosen?

I personally believe that God is longing for a reformation of the church that will take away these high places. If I understand the revelation of Scripture, our modern-day high places continually provoke God—just as He was continually provoked by the kings of Judah who worshipped Him but never removed the high places. God does not reject our worship if we meet as Baptists or Pentecostals or Lutherans or Methodists.

But I believe it provokes Him. It is not what He wants. He is waiting for the high places to be removed.

Let me follow up this thought by turning our attention to Acts 15. This chapter describes a famous meeting of leaders in the early church that was held in Jerusalem to decide how the church was to respond to Gentiles who had become believers. (Incidentally, this problem is the other way around today. Years ago, the Assemblies of God denomination held a meeting to decide whether their churches could accept Messianic believers. Eventually, one of the leaders stood up and said, "Brothers, they have accepted us—we've got to accept them!" In this way, history has come full circle.)

The controversy in Acts 15 was brought to a conclusion by James, who gave the following statement in which he quoted from the prophet Amos:

> And after they had become silent, James answered, saying, "Men and brethren, listen to me [James wasn't exactly modest; he knew he had something to say from God]: Simon [Peter] has declared how God at the first visited the Gentiles to take out of them a people for His name. And with this the words of the prophets agree, just as it is written [and here he quoted from Amos]: 'After this I will return and will rebuild the tabernacle of

> David, which has fallen down; I will rebuild its ru-
> ins, and I will set it up; so that the rest of mankind
> may seek the LORD, even all the Gentiles who are
> called by My name, says the LORD who does all
> these things.'"   (Acts 15:13–17)

The "Tabernacle of David"

Notice the central statement in the above Scripture that James quoted from Amos: *"I will return and will rebuild the tabernacle of David"*—not the tabernacle of Moses, nor the temple of Solomon, but the tabernacle of David. Where was the tabernacle of David built? In Jerusalem, the place where God had chosen to put His name. This passage gives us the scriptural basis for the whole era of the Gentile church. It is the rebuilding of the tabernacle of David.

I have heard many messages that illuminate the differences between the tabernacle of Moses and the tabernacle of David. In the tabernacle of Moses, worship was permitted only during certain hours of daylight; the tabernacle of David was open day and night. With the tabernacle of Moses, only the Levites had access; but with the tabernacle of David, there was a freedom and a spontaneity of worship—anybody could worship there.

At which kind of tabernacle are we, as God's children, able to worship? The tabernacle of David.

What was the essence of the tabernacle of David? Praise.

What was a result of the tabernacle of David? The book of Psalms.

For the Gentile church, our true charter of liberty is the rebuilding of the tabernacle of David. However, our emphasis here is not on the building but on the site where God had chosen to put His name.

In our dispensation, the key issue for us is this: Where has God chosen to put His name? The answer is not in a building, nor in a nationality, nor in a denomination, nor in a particular human leader's teachings. God has placed His name in one Person. That Person is Jesus Christ. Where are we authorized to meet? "Into" the name of Jesus. We are to gather around the invisible Person of Jesus, who meets with us when we are led together by the Spirit of God into His name.

When we repent of having turned aside to "high places" of worship, rejecting them as the basis of our meeting together as Christians, we will remove barriers that have been holding us back from fulfilling our calling as God's people in the world.

CHAPTER FOURTEEN

THE PRIMACY OF THE HOLY SPIRIT

We have established the fact that Jesus meets with us when we are led together *by the Spirit of God* into His name. We must never leave out the Holy Spirit as we gather together.

Yet, strangely enough, a major failure of the charismatic movement is that we have slighted the Holy Spirit. We talk a lot about Him—then ignore Him. We go through our rituals, our performances, and our programs, but if the Holy Spirit has a different idea, we give Him virtually no opportunity to lead us or teach us. Isn't that often true? It may be a difficult realization for us, but, like it or not, in some ways, there is no group of believers more ritualistic than charismatics. The only difference is that we do not have a *written* liturgy.

I heard a young man once say, "I started a church." I shuddered. I wanted to say to him, "You started a church? You little nincompoop! You whippersnapper! You think that you can start a church?" Nobody starts churches but Jesus and the Holy Spirit. We can organize. We can plan. We can promote. We can build. But churches are the prerogative of the Lord. He is *"head over all things to the church, which is His body"* (Ephesians 1:22–23).

As I understand Paul's teaching in Ephesians, a true church is built on a foundation of apostles and prophets who were appointed by Christ and are led by the Spirit. (See Ephesians 2:20–22; 4:11–12.) I question whether anything built on another foundation is acknowledged by God as a church. I personally believe there are hundreds of thousands of groups and buildings in America that people call churches, but that God does not recognize as such. They do not fulfill His basic requirement. It is time to let the Holy Spirit have His way.

Do you realize who the Holy Spirit is? Do you recognize that He is a Person? He has the key to the storehouse of God. All the wealth of God the Father and God the Son is administered by the Spirit. It is worthwhile making friends with Him! You can be a child of God but live like a pauper until you become friends with the Holy Spirit. He is very sensitive. Like a dove, He is easily driven away. If you develop the wrong attitude or motivation, the Dove flies off.

There is only one nature that the Dove will settle upon, and that is the nature of Jesus Christ. John the Baptist said of Jesus, *"Behold! The Lamb of God…"* (John 1:29). Then he said, *"I saw the Spirit* [of God] *descending from heaven like a dove, and He remained upon Him"* (verse 32). What is the nature of the Lamb of God? In my simple understanding, the Lamb embodies three traits: purity, meekness, and a life sacrificially laid down. The Holy Spirit will remain on a nature that has these traits.

You may be touched by the Holy Spirit one moment but, ten minutes later, find yourself far from Him, because He is choosy about where He settles. Remember what we emphasized from Matthew 18:20 in the "Prince Version": "As many as have been led by the Holy Spirit into the name of Jesus…." Jesus essentially said, "You can count on My being there, but you must meet the conditions." Our meeting place is not the baptism with the Holy Spirit or speaking in tongues or water baptism or the legacy of Luther, Calvin, Wesley, or anyone else. Our meeting place is the name of Jesus.

You may believe that what I am saying is true. The question is: What are you going to do about it? It is up to each of us to make a response to this truth.

Our Companion, Our Friend

How do we respond to this challenging matter of being led by the Holy Spirit into the name of Jesus? We get some helpful insight from Psalm 122, in which there is an amazing description of Jerusalem in just two verses:

> Jerusalem is built as a city that is compact together, where the tribes go up, the tribes of the LORD, to the Testimony of Israel, to give thanks to the name of the LORD. (Psalm 122:3–4)

The Hebrew term that is translated "compact together" is a beautiful word. It is the word from which we get the modern Hebrew word *chabar*. It means "a companion," "a close friend."

Do you see what makes Jerusalem significant? It is the place where the Lord has put His name. And when the tribes of Israel went to the city of Jerusalem three times every year, as God had commanded, they were testifying, "The Lord who dwells in Jerusalem, the Lord who has put His name in Jerusalem, is our God. That is why we all go there. Whether we are from the tribe of Benjamin or Manasseh or Ephraim is not significant. What is important is our destination—where we are headed. What is important is the place where we meet. That is the place where the Lord has set His name."

The same principle applies to us today. When we, as God's people, come together into the name of the Lord, we are testifying about who our God is. Moreover, when we are where we belong—in the place where God has put His name—and as we worship Him, we are also in the strongest and most secure place we can be to fulfill our responsibilities of waging spiritual warfare, pulling down strongholds, and defeating Satan.

CHAPTER FIFTEEN

FINDING OUR
TRUE ROOTS

As we near the conclusion of this book, let us explore one more stronghold that we need to pull down in our lives—the stronghold of holding onto our pasts. This can be a stronghold of pride in our heritage or accomplishments, or it can be a stronghold of feelings of insecurity or shame due to a negative family history or a personal failing. Either way, the past can bind us and hinder our spiritual effectiveness, if we let it.

Ancestral Roots

In the 1970s, the book *Roots: The Saga of an American Family* by Alex Haley became extremely famous and made a tremendous impact on American culture, inspiring a popular TV miniseries. The book started a movement of people searching for their own family's ancestral beginnings. Though I am British by birth, I understand why, in some ways, Americans are particularly prone to think about their roots. The United States is a land of immigrants whose roots are in many nations of the world.

I have had American friends who started to inquire into their genealogies. Then, very often, many of them would suddenly stop their search because they discovered something negative in their family tree—perhaps a relative who had been in prison or who had been charged with, or convicted of, a heinous crime.

In Australia, it is a totally different story. To be really "respectable," you have to have a convict as an ancestor! As I wrote earlier, Australia was founded as a settlement for convicts. When British officials could not send convicts to America any longer, they would send them to Australia. A resident of Tasmania, the little island south of Australia, told me quite seriously, "Everybody who is anybody here has got to have a convict as an ancestor."

My point is that people often have a strong desire to know, in general, where they come from—where their roots are—and I think God put that desire within us. Yet, when we don't like what we discover about our roots, it can influence the way we think about ourselves and even hinder our effectiveness in waging spiritual warfare.

Our Wonderful Spiritual Heritage

One of the great problems of multitudes of people today—particularly young people—is that they are rootless: They really don't know where they came from, where they belong, or where they fit in. I want to tell you that, as Christians, we have strong spiritual roots that we need to recognize. It is fine to look back to Wesley or Luther or Calvin—but that is not where our roots are. We have roots that go back a lot further in history than that.

Let us read the following passage from Romans, in which Paul was writing to Gentiles (which most of us are):

And if some of the branches [the real Israelites] *were broken off* [from their own "olive tree" by unbelief], *and you, being a wild olive tree, were grafted in among them, and with them became a partaker of the root and fatness of the olive tree, do not boast against the branches. But if you do boast, remember that you do not support the root, but the root supports you.* (Romans 11:17–18)

What Paul said is a necessary warning for the contemporary church: We must never become arrogant toward Israel. Our roots are in the patriarchs—in Abraham, Isaac, and Jacob—in their faith in God and their blessings from Him. We have a wonderful root system, one that has endured four thousand years of tumultuous history.

Did you know that no other tree lives as long as an olive tree? That is the tree Paul was talking about—the olive tree of God's chosen people founded in a man named Abraham, the father of a great multitude, the father of a new nation. You may be embarrassed about your human ancestry, but always remember that, in Jesus Christ, the old things have passed away: *"Therefore, if anyone is in Christ, he is a new creation; old things have passed away; behold, all things have become new. Now all things are of God…"* (2 Corinthians 5:17–18).

New Spiritual Ancestry

I grieve when I meet Christians who lack a sense of self-worth and security because they are not satisfied with their family backgrounds. We must realize that our natural ancestry is the *"old"* that has *"passed away."* We have been grafted in to God's own olive tree, so that we have a new spiritual ancestry. Our ancestry goes back to the men whom God chose to be the root system of a people who were to endure through history and through all ages.

A number of people do take pride or satisfaction in their natural heritage. For example, I could be satisfied with my ancestry, in the natural sense. I was born of British parents, and all of my male ancestors have been officers in the British army. But I have a much better root system than that. It is in Abraham. Consider these words:

> And he [Abraham] received the sign of circumcision, a seal of the righteousness of the faith which he had while still uncircumcised, that he might be the father of all those who believe, though they are uncircumcised [not Jews], that righteousness might be imputed to them also.   (Romans 4:11)

Who is our "*father*," if we are believers? Abraham. As a further confirmation, we read this declaration:

> And if you are Christ's, then you are Abraham's seed, and heirs according to the promise.
>   (Galatians 3:29)

We have a wonderful heritage. There is no one who can "lord it over us." You may come across aristocratic families from Europe whose ancestry goes back a thousand years. But, in Abraham, we go back four thousand years (and much further back than that in relation to the eternal plans of God). Our pedigree is traced in the Bible. That is something to be excited about. If only Christians could realize what they have become in Jesus

Christ, we wouldn't have many of the problems of insecurity and a lack of self-worth that trouble people.

Beloved by God

Let us now turn to an additional passage that reveals how deeply God cherishes us. It is found in a beautiful messianic psalm, and it is a picture of the Messiah. There is only one Person who corresponds to the person described in this psalm, and that is Jesus, the Son of God, the Messiah of Israel. It is very important for you to see this picture, because it is so wonderful:

> *My heart is overflowing with a good theme; I recite my composition concerning the King; my tongue is the pen of a ready writer.* [This next statement is addressed to the King, who is Jesus:] *You are fairer than the sons of men; grace is poured upon Your lips; therefore God has blessed You forever.*
>
> (Psalm 45:1–2)

Notice the word *"therefore."* Why did God bless Jesus? Because of the grace of His lips.

> *Gird Your sword upon Your thigh, O Mighty One, with Your glory and Your majesty. And in Your majesty ride prosperously because of truth, humility, and righteousness* [this refers to God's

King]; *and Your right hand shall teach You awesome things. Your arrows are sharp in the heart of the King's enemies; the peoples fall under You* [this refers to a conviction of sin]. *Your throne, O God, is forever and ever.* (Psalm 45:3–6)

Please notice that Jesus is addressed here as God. Oh, that the Jewish people could see that! This is the messianic King, and He is called God. Let us reread that statement as we continue:

Your throne, O God, is forever and ever; a scepter of righteousness is the scepter of Your kingdom. You love righteousness and hate wickedness; therefore God, Your God, has anointed [blessed] *You....* (Psalm 45:6–7)

These words are addressed from God to God: "God has blessed You, God." That shows us that there are at least two Persons who are called God. And why has God blessed God? Because if you *"love righteousness and hate wickedness; therefore God, Your God, has anointed* [blessed] *You."* That is one way to get blessed—to love righteousness and hate wickedness.

Therefore God, Your God, has anointed You with the oil of gladness more than Your companions. All your garments are scented with myrrh and aloes

*and cassia, out of the ivory palaces, by which they
have made You glad.* (Psalm 45:7–8)

Now, please pay careful attention to the next verse,
because it is the conclusion we have been building up to:

*Kings' daughters are among Your honorable
women; at Your right hand* [the correct place in
a Jewish marriage ceremony] *stands the queen in
gold from Ophir.* (Psalm 45:9)

Who is the queen bride? She is the church—us.
Next is the advice that relates to what I have been saying
about our search for our earthly roots:

*Listen, O daughter, consider and incline your
ear; forget your own people also, and your father's
house....* (Psalm 45:10)

The psalmist was saying, "Forget where you came
from—it's not relevant." Could that be any clearer? We
must no longer be bogged down by our nationality, our
denomination, or other aspects of our background. In
order to qualify to be the bride of Christ, we must come
out of all that.

*Forget your own people also, and your father's
house; so the King will greatly desire your beauty;*

because He is your Lord, worship Him.
(Psalm 45:10–11)

That is a picture of what Jesus wants us to be. How do we attain to it? By not placing our life's foundation or self-worth on our father's house and our own people, and by entering into our wonderful spiritual heritage.

Princes and Rulers

When God called me as a young man of about thirty, I was in what was then Palestine. I had been overseas during World War II for four and a half years, and I had the right to request that the British army send me back to Britain. However, I felt God had called me to stay in that land and serve Him there. At that point, I was torn between going back to England and seeing my parents and other family members—particularly my grandfather who was dying—or obeying the call of God.

One of the Scriptures God gave me at that time through a Christian friend was the one we have just read: *"Forget your own people also, and your father's house; so the King will greatly desire your beauty."* So I refused the right of my passage back to Britain and turned down everything I was entitled to in my secular profession at Cambridge. I gave up my background.

I could have returned to Cambridge and been a professor there for the rest of my life, having a very honorable and dignified position in the academic world. But I forsook my familial and professional background because I had been grafted into another line. I had a new root system. And I am proud of it.

The final promise we will read in Psalm 45 is found in verse 16:

> *Instead of Your fathers shall be Your sons, whom You shall make princes in all the earth.*

Let's not worry so much about the past. Let's not be so concerned about our ancestral or ecclesiastical history, or our academic or vocational accomplishments. Instead, let's focus on the fact that God will give us "sons"—His people and His work—that will become like princes, rulers for God in all the earth.

Destroy the High Places in Your Life

We have to make a decision. Are we going to stick with the high places? Are we going to maintain the places of worship that are essentially denominational? Are we going to be tied down by these things forever? Or, are we going to destroy the high places and declare that there is only one way to come together that is acceptable to God—to be led together by the Spirit of God into the name of Jesus?

It should be clear to you now that this latter step honors the Holy Spirit. It honors Jesus. It honors God the Father. When we meet on any other basis, it is not the same. Oh, God is very gracious; He is very patient—just as He was to the kings who permitted worship on the high places. But, during all that time, He was longing for a king who would carry through the reform and remove the high places.

Personally, I believe the Lord is revealing where we are situated in this move of God. We have come so far, and yet some of us have gone back to denominationalism. That is not the will of God. The will of God is to remove the high places. This does not mean you can't say, "I was a Lutheran" or "I was a Baptist" or a member of some other denomination. You can give us your history, but do not let it dictate your conduct. Forget your father's house and your own people, and the King will greatly desire your beauty. In this way, you will remove the high places that keep you from entering into your full inheritance as Christ's beloved one.

Then, as you are secure in your position in Jesus, and as you are built up in the Spirit, you will live in His love and power, and you will be able to pull down the strongholds of the enemy. As Jesus declared, *"I will build My church, and the gates of Hades shall not prevail against it"* (Matthew 16:18).

MAKING YOUR DECLARATION

In this book, we have examined two key aspects of spiritual warfare that you may not have considered before—pulling down strongholds (individual and national) and removing the high places. They represent two very important spiritual activities that will enable you to wage individual battles in spiritual warfare and to engage with fellow Christians in corporate battles as you come together in the name of Jesus, pull down national strongholds, and remove the high places.

The time has come for action. Prayer and declaration are good ways to embed in your spiritual life and destiny the principles we have examined. Will you join me in making the following declarations?

> Lord, I recognize that by virtue of my relationship with You, I have entered into active warfare with the kingdom of Satan. My first step is to declare my absolute allegiance to You,

Lord Jesus—the Captain of the Lord's host, and my Lord and Savior. I commit myself to You and Your leadership unreservedly, and I place my life fully in Your hands.

As Your Word explains, I equip myself now with the full armor of God so that I can stand victorious in this battle. I also pull down, in the name of Jesus, any stronghold or strong man in my life that hinders me. Lord Jesus, help me in this battle, so that I can follow You without obstruction.

Next, Lord, I remove any high place in my life that may be hindering me—any allegiance to an old pattern or religious practice that may be offensive to You. I lay it down now, Lord, and I place it at Your feet. I will join with my fellow believers in coming together into that one place that God the Father has authorized for worship—into the mighty and powerful name of Jesus.

Now, Lord, all that I am, and all that I have, I commit fully to You. I offer myself to You as one who will engage in spiritual warfare for the sake of Your kingdom, one who will pull down strongholds in Your name—not only individual strongholds but also national ones. And I will be one who removes the high places in my own life and in the realm of the church.

Please use me, for the sake of Your kingdom and Your eternal purposes. Amen!

About the Author

Derek Prince (1915–2003) was born in India of British parents. He was educated as a scholar of Greek and Latin at Eton College and King's College, Cambridge in England. Upon graduation he held a fellowship (equivalent to a professorship) in Ancient and Modern Philosophy at King's College. Prince also studied Hebrew, Aramaic, and modern languages at Cambridge and the Hebrew University in Jerusalem. As a student, he was a philosopher and self-proclaimed agnostic.

While in the British Medical Corps during World War II, Prince began to study the Bible as a philosophical work. Converted through a powerful encounter with Jesus Christ, he was baptized in the Holy Spirit a few days later. Out of this encounter, he formed two conclusions: first, that Jesus Christ is alive; second, that the Bible is a true, relevant, up-to-date book. These conclusions altered the whole course of his life, which he then devoted to studying and teaching the Bible as the Word of God.

Discharged from the army in Jerusalem in 1945, he married Lydia Christensen, founder of a children's home there. Upon their marriage, he immediately became father to Lydia's eight adopted daughters—six Jewish, one Palestinian Arab, and one English. Together, the family saw the rebirth of the state of Israel in 1948. In the late 1950s, they adopted another daughter while Prince was serving as principal of a teacher training college in Kenya.

In 1963, the Princes immigrated to the United States and pastored a church in Seattle. In 1973, Prince became one of the founders of Intercessors for America. His book *Shaping History through Prayer and Fasting* has awakened Christians around the world to their responsibility to pray for their governments. Many consider underground translations of the book as instrumental in the fall of communist regimes in the USSR, East Germany, and Czechoslovakia.

Lydia Prince died in 1975, and Prince married Ruth Baker (a single mother to three adopted children) in 1978. He met his second wife, like his first wife, while she was serving the Lord in Jerusalem. Ruth died in December 1998 in Jerusalem, where they had lived since 1981.

Until a few years before his own death in 2003 at the age of eighty-eight, Prince persisted in the ministry

God had called him to as he traveled the world, imparting God's revealed truth, praying for the sick and afflicted, and sharing his prophetic insights into world events in the light of Scripture. Internationally recognized as a Bible scholar and spiritual patriarch, Derek Prince established a teaching ministry that spanned six continents and more than sixty years. He is the author of more than fifty books, six hundred audio teachings, and one hundred video teachings, many of which have been translated and published in more than one hundred languages. He pioneered teaching on such groundbreaking themes as generational curses, the biblical significance of Israel, and demonology.

Prince's radio program, which began in 1979, has been translated into more than a dozen languages and continues to touch lives. Derek's main gift of explaining the Bible and its teaching in a clear and simple way has helped build a foundation of faith in millions of lives. His nondenominational, nonsectarian approach has made his teaching equally relevant and helpful to people from all racial and religious backgrounds, and his teaching is estimated to have reached more than half the globe.

In 2002, he said, "It is my desire—and I believe the Lord's desire—that this ministry continue the work which God began through me over sixty years ago, until Jesus returns."

Derek Prince Ministries International continues to reach out to believers in over 140 countries with Derek's teachings, fulfilling the mandate to keep on "until Jesus returns." This is accomplished through the outreaches of more than forty-five Derek Prince offices around the world, including primary work in Australia, Canada, China, France, Germany, the Netherlands, New Zealand, Norway, Russia, South Africa, Switzerland, the United Kingdom, and the United States. For current information about these and other worldwide locations, visit www.derekprince.com.